# The Hope of Christmas with Pope Francis

### by Amette Ley

*All booklets are published thanks to the
generous support of the members of the
Catholic Truth Society*

### CATHOLIC TRUTH SOCIETY
PUBLISHERS TO THE HOLY SEE

# Contents

*All rights reserved. First published 2017 by The Incorporated Catholic Truth Society, 40-46 Harleyford Road, London SE11 5AY Tel: 020 7640 0042 Fax: 020 7640 0046. © 2017 The Incorporated Catholic Truth Society.*

*ISBN 978 1 78469 196 7*

# Introduction

*In this Season of Advent, which is the time
of waiting, in which we prepare ourselves to
welcome once again the comforting mystery of the
Incarnation and the light of Christmas,
it is important to reflect on hope.
Let us allow the Lord to teach us
what it means to hope.*[1]

(Pope Francis)

In this booklet we follow the teachings of Pope Francis as we prepare for the birth of the Lord Jesus through the theme of hope.

We see how this hope was present from the very beginning, shining through the horror of the Fall with the promise of a Saviour: "After the fall, [God] buoyed them up with the hope of salvation, by promising redemption; and he has never ceased to show his solicitude for the human race" (*Catechism of the Catholic Church* (*CCC*), 55). This hope was never diminished, though God's people went through captivity and exile, suffering the consequences of forgetting God's covenant with them from time to time, but never completely losing their hope.

We note how that hope culminated not in great power or riches, but in a young girl whose life was hidden from the powerful. She was the flower of Israel and the hope of the nations.

With the Resurrection, our hope is confirmed, and the Church looks forward to the time when Christ will return in glory, living in the hope and expectation of that day. Pope Francis reminds us of that "last visit, which we proclaim each time that we recite the Creed: 'He will come again in glory to judge the living and the dead'".[2]

However, this hope is not only for members of the Church; it is for the whole world. Benedict XVI understood this well: "Christians…in the context of their knowledge and experience, must learn anew in what their hope truly consists, what they have to offer to the world and what they cannot offer."[3]

Finally, we see how "Christmas has above all a taste of hope because, for all the darkness in our lives, God's light shines forth":[4]

> For I know the plans I have for you, says the Lord, plans for welfare and not for evil, to give you a future and a hope. (*Jr* 29:11)

# HOPE OF ISRAEL - FIRST WEEK OF ADVENT

## Prayers and readings

Give us the grace, Lord, to be ever on the watch for Christ your Son. When he comes and knocks at our door, let him find us alert in prayer, joyfully proclaiming his glory. Through our Lord Jesus Christ, your Son, who lives and reigns with you and the Holy Spirit, one God, for ever and ever.

*(Evening Prayer, Monday of the first week of Advent)*

O my God, relying on Your almighty power and infinite mercy and promises, I hope to obtain pardon for my sins, the help of Your grace, and life everlasting, through the merits of Jesus Christ, my Lord and Redeemer.

*(Act of Hope)*

Behold, the eye of the Lord is on those who fear him,
on those who hope in his steadfast love,
that he may deliver their soul from death,
and keep them alive in famine.
Our soul waits for the Lord; he is our help and shield.
Yes, our heart is glad in him,
because we trust in his holy name.
Let your steadfast love, O Lord, be upon us,
even as we hope in you. *(Ps 33:18-22)*

Beloved, now is the acceptable time spoken of by the Spirit, the day of salvation, peace and reconciliation: the great season of Advent. This is the time eagerly awaited by the patriarchs and prophets, the time that holy Simeon rejoiced at last to see. This is the season that the Church has always celebrated with special solemnity. We too should always observe it with faith and love, offering praise and thanksgiving to the Father for the mercy and love he has shown us in this mystery. In his infinite love for us, though we were sinners, he sent his only Son to free us from the tyranny of Satan, to summon us to heaven, to welcome us into its innermost recesses, to show us truth itself, to train us in right conduct, to plant within us the seeds of virtue, to enrich us with the treasures of his grace, and to make us children of God and heirs of eternal life.

*(Second Reading, Office of Readings,*
*Monday of the first week of Advent[5])*

### Hope at the beginning

From the very beginning of Creation, even before the people of Israel were formed as a people for God, humanity had a great hope in the goodness of the Lord. Whatever the exact nature of the moral event which we now call the Fall, the effects of man's disobedience to, and subsequent rift from, his Creator, were catastrophic, reverberating down the centuries and still affecting humanity today.

Surely those first human beings felt the hopelessness we sometimes experience as Pope Francis describes it:

> We have such need, in these times which appear dark, in which we sometimes feel disoriented at the evil and violence which surrounds us, at the distress of so many of our brothers and sisters. We need hope! We feel disoriented and even rather discouraged, because we are powerless and it seems this darkness will never end.[6]

The woman, Eve, we are told, found many reasons for her disobedience. She saw, as women often see initially, a practical use for the tree. It was good for food. It would feed her and her husband, and perhaps she looked forward to the family she might have. Next, she noticed how beautiful it was. Of course it was beautiful, as God had created it. She must have instantly loved it. And finally, she looked at the future and how it might be. This fruit would make her wise, and her husband too. This was her hope - a hope which was good: food for the family, something beautiful and attractive, and the overwhelming hope of wisdom in the future. Good hopes - but disordered, as would be the consequence of this disobedience down the ages. We hope for good things, but our hopes are disordered and we put our own plans before the Wisdom of God.

> So when the woman saw that the tree was good for food, and that it was a delight to the eyes, and that the tree was to be desired to make one wise, she took of its

fruit and ate; and she also gave some to her husband, and he ate. (*Gn* 3:6)

Pope Francis expresses it thus:

The Book of Genesis shows us the first no, the original "no", the human "no", when man preferred to gaze upon himself rather than on his Creator; he wanted to go his own way, and chose to be self-sufficient. However, in so doing, forsaking communion with God, he lost his own self and began to fear, to hide himself and to accuse those who were close by (cf. *Gn* 3:10, 12). These are symptoms: fear is always a symptom of a "no" to God, and indicates that I am saying "no" to God; accusing others and not looking at ourselves indicates that I am distancing myself from God. This is the sin. Yet, the Lord does not leave man at the mercy of his sin; immediately he looks for him, and asks a question that is full of apprehension: "Where are you?"

However, even in the midst of such upheaval and tragedy, humanity was not without hope. God speaks to the serpent whom we take to be Satan, the enemy of humanity, the fallen angel who would not serve:

I will put enmity between you and the woman,
and between your seed and her seed;
he shall bruise your head,
and you shall bruise his heel. (*Gn* 3:15)

The Church has seen a great hope in these words and an early promise of salvation, calling them the *Protoevangelion*, or 'first gospel'.[7] It is "the first announcement of the Messiah and Redeemer, of a battle between the serpent and the Woman, and of the final victory of a descendant of hers" (*CCC*, 410).

The *Catechism* continues:

> The Christian tradition sees in this passage an announcement of the "New Adam" who, because he "became obedient unto death, even death on a cross", makes amends superabundantly for the disobedience of Adam. Furthermore many Fathers and Doctors of the Church have seen the woman announced in the Protoevangelium as Mary, the mother of Christ, the "new Eve". Mary benefited first of all and uniquely from Christ's victory over sin: she was preserved from all stain of original sin and by a special grace of God committed no sin of any kind during her whole earthly life. (*CCC*, 411)

During Advent we celebrate the Solemnity of the Immaculate Conception of Mary. This has everything to do with this early promise of salvation and the events surrounding it, but can also be a source of great confusion in the world as it is sometimes understood as the conception of Jesus in Mary's womb by the power of the Holy Spirit. The misunderstanding arises from a misconception that the

Church does not approve of sexual relations and therefore sees a conception without them as very good, without sin, or "immaculate". This is not the case. The Church holds sexual union in such high regard as the reflection of God's covenant with humanity and the means by which we share in his creative work that she is insistent that it be reserved for marriage.

The Immaculate Conception does not refer to the conception of Jesus at all, but rather to the conception of Mary in her own mother's womb.[8] This was not a conception without normal human intercourse; Mary was conceived in the same way as most people. "Immaculate" refers to the Church's understanding that Mary was conceived, was born, and lived her life without the burden of Original Sin or personal sin which all other human beings, except for the Lord Jesus, must carry. Like Eve, who was also free from Original Sin at the time of her fall, Mary had to be perfectly free to choose to co-operate with God's plan. St Bernard highlights the significance of this freedom:

> The angel awaits your reply, for it is time that he should return to God, Who sent him. We too are waiting, O Lady, for a word of mercy we, who are groaning under the sentence of condemnation. See, the price of our salvation is offered to you; if you consent, we shall at once be delivered. By the Eternal Word of God we were all created, and behold we die. By your short answer we shall be refreshed and recalled to life. Adam, with all his

race[,] Adam, a weeping exile from Paradise, implores it of you. Abraham entreats you, David beseeches you. This is the object of the burning desires of the holy fathers, of your fathers, who are still dwelling in the region of the shades of death. Behold the entire human race prostrate at your feet in expectation.

And rightly, for on your word depend the consolation of the wretched, the redemption of the captive, the freedom of the condemned, the salvation of your entire race, of all the children of Adam. Hasten, then, O Lady, to give your answer; hasten to speak the word so longed for by all on earth.[9]

Pope Francis also reminds us of this as he points out:

In the Gospel, with one word only, she is called "full of grace" (*Lk* 1:28), that is, filled with grace. It means that, in her, full of grace from the start, there is no space for sin. And when we turn to her, we too recognise this beauty: we invoke her, "full of grace", without a shadow of evil.[10]

## Hope in a fallen world

As time passed, the consequences of sin were many, but the hope offered by God never failed. Pope Francis reminds us that,

particularly in this Season of Advent, which is the time of waiting, in which we prepare ourselves to welcome once again the comforting mystery of the Incarnation and the light of Christmas, it is important to reflect on hope.[11]

The narrative of Noah and the flood provides a wonderful picture of hope for us. Humanity has made many mistakes and is in a position of what is, humanly speaking, complete hopelessness. God has decided to destroy life.

> The Lord saw that the wickedness of man was great in the earth, and that every imagination of the thoughts of his heart was only evil continually. And the Lord was sorry that he had made man on the earth, and it grieved him to his heart. So the Lord said, "I will blot out man whom I have created from the face of the ground, man and beast and creeping things and birds of the air, for I am sorry that I have made them." But Noah found favour in the eyes of the Lord. (*Gn* 6:5-8)

The Lord, who is life itself and the author of all life, will not destroy the life he has created. The Ark is perhaps the most powerful symbol of hope in the entire Old Testament. It is a prefiguration of the Church in which all can take refuge from the storms caused by sin. It is a prefiguration of our Christian Baptism, in which lies all our hope.

> God's patience waited in the days of Noah, during the building of the ark, in which a few, that is, eight persons, were saved through water. Baptism, which corresponds to this, now saves you, not as a removal of dirt from the body but as an appeal to God for a clear

conscience, through the resurrection of Jesus Christ, who has gone into heaven and is at the right hand of God, with angels, authorities, and powers subject to him. (*1 P* 3:20-22)

Together with the Ark is the symbol of the rainbow[12] to which God directs Noah and his family. When they see this - as no doubt they had seen it many times before - they were to remember that it now had a new meaning of hope. A covenant is created between God and man, and a sure and certain hope is established.

Then God said to Noah and to his sons with him, "Behold, I establish my covenant with you and your descendants after you, and with every living creature that is with you, the birds, the cattle, and every beast of the earth with you, as many as came out of the ark. I establish my covenant with you, that never again shall all flesh be cut off by the waters of a flood, and never again shall there be a flood to destroy the earth." And God said, "This is the sign of the covenant which I make between me and you and every living creature that is with you, for all future generations: I set my bow in the cloud, and it shall be a sign of the covenant between me and the earth. When I bring clouds over the earth and the bow is seen in the clouds, I will remember my covenant which is between me and you and every living creature of all flesh; and the waters shall never again become a flood to destroy all flesh. When the bow is in the clouds, I will look upon it and remember the everlasting covenant between God and every living creature of all flesh that is upon the earth." God said to Noah, "This is the sign of the covenant which I have established between me and all flesh that is upon the earth." (*Gn* 9: 8-17)

## Hope in a new beginning

Hope is one of the theological virtues (the others are faith and charity) which enable us to live in relationship with God the Holy Trinity.

[T]he theological virtues…adapt man's faculties for participation in the divine nature: for the[y] relate directly to God. They dispose Christians to live in a relationship with the Holy Trinity. They have the One and Triune God for their origin, motive and object.

The theological virtues are the foundation of Christian moral activity; they animate it and give it its special character. They inform and give life to all the moral virtues. They are infused by God into the souls of the faithful to make them capable of acting as his children and of meriting eternal life. They are the pledge of the presence and action of the Holy Spirit in the faculties of the human being. There are three theological virtues: faith, hope, and charity. (*CCC*, 1812-1813)

These virtues were what impelled Abraham to leave his country and journey to where God asked him to be; through love of God he obeyed, through great faith in God he did as he was asked - even to believing he would have a son when he and his wife were well past the age and then offering that son as a sacrifice - and through hope in God's promises he saw those promises fulfilled. Pope Francis says:

> Trusting in the Lord's word that a son would be born to him, Abraham left his home for a new land. Although the fulfilment of God's promise was long delayed and seemed to be impossible, Abraham continued to hope. Even his discouragement and complaints were a sign of his continuing trust in God. Abraham, our father in faith, shows us that sure trust in God's word does not mean that we will not have moments of uncertainty, disappointment and bewilderment. It was at such a moment that God appeared to Abraham, called him forth from his tent and showed him the night sky shining with countless stars, assuring him that such would be the number of his descendants. Hope is always directed to the future, to the fulfilment of God's promises. May the example of Abraham teach us not be afraid to go out from our own tents, our limited outlooks, and to lift our eyes to the stars.[13]

God's covenant with Abraham was more extensive than that with Noah; more than the promise of peace for an extended family, God now expanded the hope he offered to Abraham and promised that he would be the founder of a great people.

I will indeed bless you, and I will multiply your descendants as the stars of heaven and as the sand which is on the seashore. (*Gn* 22:17)

We see this hope fulfilled throughout the Old Testament as Abraham's family grows and becomes prosperous. However, the fallen-ness of human nature arises again and again and we find this family, the recipients of so much care and promise, living as captives in the land of Egypt as a result of a cruel action by Joseph's jealous brothers. God turns this despair to hope - the greatest hope of all - through the Passover and the Exodus from Egypt, one of the defining moments of salvation history. The courage needed for this escape, and the hope which sustained it, are still needed today, in the Church and in each individual Christian. Pope Francis outlines the internal difficulties we face in saying "yes" to this hope:

For each of us too, there is a history of salvation made up of "yeses" and "nos". Sometimes, though, we are experts in the half-hearted "yes": we are good at pretending not to understand what God wants and what our conscience suggests. We are also crafty and so as not to say a true "no" to God, we say: "Sorry, I can't"; "Not today, I think tomorrow"; "Tomorrow I'll be better; tomorrow I will pray, I will do good tomorrow". And this cunning leads us away from the "yes". It distances us from God and leads us to "no", to the sinful "no", to the "no" of mediocrity. The famous "yes, but..."; "yes, Lord, but...". In this way we close the door to goodness, and evil takes advantage of these omitted "yeses". Each of us has a collection of them within. Think about it: we will find many omitted "yeses". ...Every "yes" to God gives rise to stories of salvation for us and for others.[14]

## Hope in times of trouble

The escape from Egypt was not without its troubles. The people were free, but they found it difficult to hope. Wandering in the desert, they complained to their leader Moses:

> And the whole congregation of the people of Israel murmured against Moses and Aaron in the wilderness, and said to them, "Would that we had died by the hand of the Lord in the land of Egypt, when we sat by the fleshpots and ate bread to the full; for you have brought us out into this wilderness to kill this whole assembly with hunger." (*Ex* 16:2-3)

Pope Francis observes:

> Life is often a desert, it is difficult to walk in life, but if
> we trust in God it can become beautiful and wide as a
> highway. Just never lose hope, just continue to believe,
> always, in spite of everything. When we are before a
> child, although we have many problems and many
> difficulties, a smile comes to us from within, because
> we see hope in front of us: a child is hope! And in this
> way we must be able to discern in life the way of hope
> which leads us to find God, God who became a Child for
> us. He will make us smile, he will give us everything![15]

In spite of themselves, God's people reached the Promised
Land across the river Jordan - another prefiguration of
our salvation through the waters of Baptism. They settled
there, but their hopes for the future were still disordered.
They were not content with God as their ruler and insisted
on having a king like the surrounding nations did. This did
not work out too well; Saul, the first king, was a troubled
soul and did not always lead well, David, who succeeded
him, turned out to be a weak and sinful character, and his
son Solomon allowed his many wives to bring their idols
into the temple he had built to the Lord. Soon the kingdom
was split into two and hope was obscured as rival nations
began to surround and conquer. The northern part of the
kingdom and then the southern part were overcome and
their people led away into exile in Assyria and Babylon.

There they had time to reflect on their situation and what hope there might be for the future.

Pope Francis reminds us of the words of the prophet Isaiah, "the great prophet of Advent":

> Comfort, comfort my people, says your God. Speak tenderly to Jerusalem, and cry to her that her warfare is ended, that her iniquity is pardoned.... "A voice cries: In the wilderness prepare the way of the Lord, make straight in the desert a highway for our God. Every valley shall be lifted up, and every mountain and hill be made low; the uneven ground shall become level, and the rough places a plain. And the glory of the Lord shall be revealed, and all flesh shall see it together, for the mouth of the Lord has spoken". (*Is* 40:1-2, 3-5)

The emphasis here is on the comfort God will send, reminding us of the comfort we need before we can begin to hope again. As Pope Francis puts it:

> God the Father comforts by raising up comforters, whom he asks to encourage the people, his children, by proclaiming that the tribulation has ended, affliction has ended, and sins have been forgiven. This is what heals the afflicted and fearful heart. This is why the Prophet asks them to prepare the way of the Lord, to be ready to receive his gifts and his salvation.[16]

However, the prophets were not always seen as comforters, especially those who spoke the word of God around the time of the Exile. For example, Jeremiah speaks this stern warning to God's people when he realises they have no intention of changing their wicked ways:

> Thus says the Lord: Behold, I set before you the way of life and the way of death. He who stays in this city shall die by the sword, by famine, and by pestilence; but he who goes out and surrenders to the Chaldeans who are besieging you shall live and shall have his life as a prize of war. For I have set my face against this city for evil and not for good, says the Lord: it shall be given into the hand of the king of Babylon, and he shall burn it with fire. (*Jr* 21:8-10)

At last the seventy years of exile were over and the people began to return to their own land; desolate and ruined as it was, they were filled with joy that their hopes of return were fulfilled. Pope Francis says:

> The Exile was a fraught moment in the history of Israel, when the people had lost everything. The people had lost their homeland, freedom, dignity, and even trust in God. They felt abandoned and hopeless. Instead, however, there is the Prophet's appeal which reopens the heart to faith. The desert is a place in which it is difficult to live, but precisely there, one can now walk in order to return not only to the homeland, but return to God, and return to hoping and smiling.[17]

## Hope of a Messiah

All through the long years of exile and before that, the hope which God gave to his people burned steadily, sometimes brighter, sometimes dimmed, but always present. Slowly, the idea of a Person who would be sent by God to save his people began to emerge from the diverse strands of hope. From the promise that the serpent's head would be bruised, through the hope of safety and blessing of Noah, and the unfocused but solemn promise of blessing to Abraham and his descendants, the idea materialises of a single person; one who is royal, in the line of David; a person who will establish peace and prosperity in the land. Many themes from the Old Testament mingle together to produce this hope of a Saviour, an Anointed One, and even a Servant who will suffer for the sins of others.

He was despised and rejected by men,
a man of sorrows, and acquainted with grief,
and as one from whom men hide their faces
he was despised, and we esteemed him not.
Surely he has borne our griefs
and carried our sorrows;
yet we esteemed him stricken,
smitten by God, and afflicted.
But he was wounded for our transgressions, he was
bruised for our iniquities;
upon him was the chastisement that made us whole,
and with his stripes we are healed.

All we like sheep have gone astray;
we have turned every one to his own way;
and the Lord has laid on him
the iniquity of us all. (*Is* 53:3-6)

This hope and expectation was at its highest point when John the Baptist began his preaching in the desert. Pope Francis says:

When the Baptist proclaims Jesus' coming, it is as if the Israelites are still in exile, because they are under the Roman dominion, which renders them foreigners in their own homeland, ruled by powerful occupiers that make decisions about their lives. …

…[The] very words of Isaiah were…used by John the Baptist in his preaching that invites to conversion. This is what he said: "The voice of one crying in the wilderness: Prepare the way of the Lord" (*Mt* 3:3). It is a voice which cries out where it seems that no one can hear it - for who can listen in the desert? - and which cries out in the disorientation caused by a crisis of faith. We cannot deny that the world today is in a crisis of faith. One says: "I believe in God, I am a Christian" - "I belong to this religion...". But your life is far from being Christian; it is far removed from God! Religion, faith is but an expression: "Do I believe?" - "Yes!" This means returning to God, converting the heart to God and going on this path to find him. He is waiting for us. This is

John the Baptist's preaching: prepare. Prepare for the encounter with this Child…[18]

When John the Baptist pointed to Jesus and said, "Behold the Lamb of God who takes away the sins of the world" (*Jn* 1:29), he was articulating the hope of Israel in its highest form, the fusion of the concepts developed throughout Israel's long relationship with God; Son of God, Anointed One, King from David's line and servant, like a lamb offering no resistance but suffering for the sins of others.

## Points to ponder

- "Where are you?" God called to Adam (*Gn* 3:9). As we begin our preparation during Advent in order to celebrate the joy of Christmas, pause for a moment and hear that question for yourself. Where are you in your walk with God as you read these words?

- You stand in a long line of those whom God has prepared to receive this hope; you are reading this today because others have held this hope and passed it on. Who were those others who have led and guided you through life so that you are today reading about Advent and hope and joy?

- Who are those to whom you wish to pass on some part of this hope? Is your life a witness for them to the hope that is in you?

### A prayer for those who have guided us to hope, and for those we try to guide

Lord God, you have entered our history in order to free us from the slavery of sin, you set your tent among us to share our existence, you heal our wounds and give us new life with joy and hope. Bless, we implore you, those who have guided us on the path of hope and grant that they may always travel with you and rest in peace with you at the last. Bless also those who look to us for guidance and hope. Give us the strength to witness by our lives and our words to the hope that is in us as we prepare during this Advent to celebrate the birth of your Son. We ask this through Jesus Christ our Lord. Amen.[19]

# HOPE OF MARY - SECOND WEEK OF ADVENT

*The glories of Mary are for the sake of Jesus...*
*[W]e praise and bless her as the first of creatures, that*
*we may duly confess Him as our sole Creator.*[20]

(Cardinal John Henry Newman)

### Prayers and readings

May the splendour of your glory dawn in our hearts,
we pray, almighty God,
that all shadows of the night may be scattered
and we may be shown to be children of light
by the advent of your Only Begotten Son.
Who lives and reigns with you in the unity of the Holy
Spirit, one God, for ever and ever.

*(Collect, Saturday of the second week of Advent)*

I pray, O dearest Mother, that through your most powerful
intercession my heart may be filled with Holy Hope, so that
in life's darkest hour I may never fail to trust in God my
Saviour, but by walking in the way of His commandments
I may merit to be united with Him, and with you in the
eternal joys of Heaven. Amen.
Mary, our Hope, have pity on us.
Hope of the Hopeless, pray for us.[21]

O Mary, help us your children to be men and women of hope! Help us remember that imperishable inheritance being kept for us in heaven. Help us remember that if we suffer with Christ here on earth, we will also one day be glorified with Him in heaven. O Mary, Mother of Divine Hope, keep this joy set before us, so that we can faithfully carry our cross with Christ, and bring many souls with us to heaven. Amen.[22]

Blessed is she who believed that there would be a fulfilment of what was spoken to her from the Lord. (*Lk* 1:35)

The Lord, coming into his own creation in visible form, was sustained by his own creation which he himself sustains in being. His obedience on the tree of the cross reversed the disobedience at the tree in Eden; the good news of the truth announced by an angel to Mary, a virgin subject to a husband, undid the evil lie that seduced Eve, a virgin espoused to a husband.

As Eve was seduced by the word of an angel and so fled from God after disobeying his word, Mary in her turn was given the good news by the word of an angel, and bore God in obedience to his word. As Eve was seduced into disobedience to God, so Mary was persuaded into obedience to God; thus the Virgin Mary became the advocate of the virgin Eve.

Christ gathered all things into one, by gathering them into himself. He declared war against our enemy, crushed him who at the beginning had taken us captive in Adam, and trampled on his head, in accordance with God's words to the serpent in Genesis: I will put enmity between you and the woman, and between your seed and her seed; he shall lie in wait for your head, and you shall lie in wait for his heel.

The one lying in wait for the serpent's head is the one who was born in the likeness of Adam from the woman, the Virgin. …The enemy would not have been defeated fairly if his vanquisher had not been born of a woman, because it was through a woman that he had gained mastery over man in the beginning, and set himself up as man's adversary.

That is why the Lord proclaims himself the Son of Man, the one who renews in himself that first man from whom the race born of woman was formed; as by a man's defeat our race fell into the bondage of death, so by a man's victory we were to rise again to life.

*(Second Reading, Office of Readings,*
*Friday of the second week of Advent*[23])

Hail Holy Queen, Mother of Mercy;
Hail our life, our sweetness and our hope!
To you do we cry, poor banished children of Eve;
To you do we send up our sighs,
    mourning and weeping in this vale of tears.
Turn then, most gracious advocate,
    your eyes of mercy towards us,
And after this our exile,
    show unto us the blessed fruit of your womb, Jesus.
O clement, O loving, O sweet Virgin Mary.
Pray for us O holy Mother of God.
That we may be made worthy of the promises of Christ.

*(The Hail Holy Queen)*

## Mary - flower of Israel's hope

Throughout the Old Covenant the mission of many holy women *prepared* for that of Mary. ...Mary "stands out among the poor and humble of the Lord, who confidently hope for and receive salvation from him. After a long period of waiting the times are fulfilled in her, the exalted Daughter of Sion, and the new plan of salvation is established." (*CCC*, 489)

Pope Francis speaks of the history of "God's little ones", supposedly weak and powerless, but who had their part to play in the great history of our salvation.

[T]he true history is not the one made by the powerful, but the one made by God together with his little ones. The true history - that which will remain in eternity - is the one that God writes with his little ones: God with Mary, God with Jesus, God with Joseph, God with the little ones. Those little and simple people whom we see around the new-born Jesus: Zechariah and Elizabeth, who were old and barren, Mary, the young virgin maiden betrothed to Joseph, the shepherds, who were scorned and counted for nothing. It is the little ones, made great by their faith, the little ones who are able to continue to hope.[24]

These "little ones" of God are examples of the hope that Advent holds; many years before the promise was fulfilled, they hoped in God and acted accordingly, though their circumstances would have suggested neither hope nor virtue in some cases. We think of Eve, with everything lost and bereft of any comfort, yet she receives the first promise of hope. She will have a descendant who will triumph over Satan and she is the mother of all the living. In spite of her sin, and that of Adam, God does not leave them without hope. Pope Francis reminds us that, as soon as we sin, God is already leading us to repentance and salvation.

[T]he Lord does not leave man at the mercy of his sin; immediately he looks for him, and asks a question that is full of apprehension: "Where are you?"...It is as if he is saying: "Stop, think: where are you?" It is the question of a father or a mother looking for a lost child: "Where are you? What situation have you gotten yourself into?" And God does this with great patience, to the point of bridging the gap which arose from the origin.[25]

This is an important theme of Advent; to become aware of the greatness of God's mercy as he calls us, even as we sin, "Where are you?" As we wait in hope for the birth of the Christ child and for his return in glory, we wait with the assurance that God has not abandoned us - not as individuals, nor as the Church nor as the whole human race. He constantly calls us, asking "Where are you?" Advent is our opportunity to ask ourselves the same question. Where are we? Where am I?

The character of Eve shows us the deepest despair possible resulting from the loss of communion between God and mankind; surely no human being could have committed a more significant sin with such far-reaching consequences, except perhaps Judas. Yet it is to this woman that the most extensive and far-reaching promises are made, even as she leaves the paradise created for her. Surely God's mercy extends so far beyond our human failings that no sin of which we repent is beyond his saving grace. To Mary also, a promise of enormous magnitude and significance is made; she is the second Eve who will reverse the disobedience and bring hope to the world.

We hear also of Sarah, the wife of Abraham, who is promised a child, though she is well past child-bearing age. How incredulous Sarah was when she heard this promise. It seemed impossible, ridiculous, to her that she could conceive at her stage of life. When she, from inside the tent, heard the angelic visitors speak of it, her reaction was to laugh, as Abraham had done earlier. Yet, in spite of her laughter, Sarah had a sense of who was offering her this hope. She was not an influential and powerful woman. For years she had carried the burden of barrenness, she had suffered her husband asking her to lie about their relationship to Pharaoh in Egypt, and had gone through the humiliation of seeing her maid conceive a son by her husband at her own suggestion. And after such a life of shame and disgrace, Sarah hears this promise of hope. No wonder she laughs - but she also believes and hopes, and the following year she does indeed give birth to Isaac, whose name refers to laughter. Mary also was not physically capable of bearing a child at the time of the Angel's visit, being a virgin. Perhaps the story of Sarah flashed through her mind when the Angel delivered God's news to her. Steeped in the history of Israel, did she begin to understand her place as the culmination of the hopes of these holy women who played a partial role?

Pope Francis reminds us:

Every "yes" to God gives rise to stories of salvation for us and for others. Like Mary with her own "yes". In this Advent journey, God wishes to visit us and awaits our "yes".[26]

The *Catechism of the Catholic Church* (489) reminds us of many other women who were considered weak and powerless, but who believed and hoped in God who is faithful to his promises.

Hannah, the mother of Samuel the prophet, also suffered greatly over her inability to conceive; discriminated against by her husband and tormented by his other wife who did have children, she could only have recourse to hope and to prayer. How difficult it must have been for her to hope, but her prayers were heard and Samuel was born and promised to God. We see here a foreshadowing of Mary's joy in the Lord as Hannah pronounces a great hymn of hope and thanksgiving (cf. *1 S* 2:1-10) which Mary's Magnificat takes up and echoes so long afterwards. Surely Our Blessed Lady would have thought of Hannah as she lifted up her voice to God in thanksgiving and praise.

The story of Deborah also prefigures the motherhood of Mary, as she is called "Mother in Israel" (*Jg* 5:7). Uniquely in the history of Israel, Deborah is a leader, a "judge", to whom problems are brought and by whom decisions are made. After the victory of the Israelites against the

Canaanites, Deborah also sings a song - a song of victory as Miriam sang after the Red Sea crossing.

Ruth, widowed and destitute in a foreign land, yet faithful in hope to her mother-in-law; Judith, widowed and angry at her people for their lack of resistance, who herself kills the leader of the Assyrians; and Esther, an orphan living in exile who spoke up for her people at the risk of her own life - all these women, and many more, were mostly not possessed of great physical strength or power and influence, but they had hope, and the strands of their hope filter down through the development and spiritual flourishing of the Jewish people to meet in Mary, the flower of Israel. Mary is the Second Eve, the virgin, the mother of a prophet, the Mother in Israel who leads God's people to victory, faithful in hope and great intercessor for us with her Son. But above all, Mary is the one who was able to say an unqualified "Yes" to God. As Pope Francis expresses it:

> Mary responds to God's proposal by saying: "Behold, I am the handmaid of the Lord"... She does not say: "Well, this time I will do God's will; I will make myself available, then I will see..." No. Hers is a full, total "yes", for her entire life, without conditions. And just as the original "no" closed the passage between man and God, so Mary's "yes" opened the path to God among us. It is the most important "yes" in history, the humble

"yes" which reverses the prideful original "no", the faithful "yes" that heals disobedience, the willing "yes" that overturns the vanity of sin.[27]

## Mary - hope in God

Pope Francis reminds us that "[o]ur hope is not a concept, it is not a sentiment…it is not a heap of riches! Our hope is a Person, it is the Lord Jesus whom we recognise as living and present in us and in our brothers, because Christ is risen."[28] Pope Benedict taught the same, referring to the "encounter with an event, a person, which gives life a new horizon and a decisive direction".[29] "Mary is a woman of hope: only because she believes in God's promises and awaits the salvation of Israel, can the angel visit her and call her to the decisive service of these promises."[30]

The Church defines hope in this way:

Hope is the theological virtue by which we desire the Kingdom of heaven and eternal life as our happiness, placing our trust in Christ's promises and relying not on our own strength, but on the help of the grace of the Holy Spirit. "Let us hold fast the confession of our hope without wavering, for he who promised is faithful." "The Holy Spirit…he poured out upon us richly through Jesus Christ our Saviour, so that we might be justified by his grace and become heirs in hope of eternal life." (*CCC*, 1817)

This is how Mary hoped. Like most of her countrymen, she hoped for the salvation of Israel - in the person of a Messiah, an anointed one who would bring the fulfilment of the hopes of the nation. She placed her trust in the promises of God because this was her 'default position'; she was accustomed, through the singular grace God had given her, to trusting in God and thus was open to receive all the graces he bestowed on her. This was possible not through her own strength, but through her reliance on the Holy Spirit, who brought to her the grace to hope.

We see the expression of Mary's hope in her question to the Angel at the Annunciation: "How can that be, since I have no knowledge of man?" (*Lk* 1:34). This is not the doubting question of Zechariah to the Angel, "By what sign am I to be assured of this?" (*Lk* 1:18), but the natural questioning of a human mind seeking to ponder more deeply the mystery of God. It is the question of a woman who lives in hope, who has already given her assent, accepted the task, and who seeks to immerse herself further in the mystery of faith.

Pope Francis sees the beauty and grace in Mary as she makes this answer.

Because of this "yes" Jesus began his journey along the path of humanity; he began it in Mary, spending the first months of life in his mother's womb: he did not appear as a man, grown and strong, but he followed the journey of a human being. He was made equal to us in every way, except one thing, that "no". Except sin. For this reason, he chose Mary, the only creature without sin, immaculate. In the Gospel, with one word only, she is called "full of grace" (*Lk* 1:28), that is, filled with grace. It means that, in her, full of grace from the start, there is no space for sin. And when we turn to her, we too recognise this beauty: we invoke her, "full of grace", without a shadow of evil.[31]

[W]e look to Mary, Mother of hope. With her "yes" she opened the door of our world to God: her maiden's heart was full of hope, wholly enlivened by faith; and thus God chose her and she believed in his word. She…for nine months was the Ark of the new and eternal Covenant.[32]

## Mary - sustained by hope

The symbol of hope has traditionally been an anchor, symbolising how we are anchored to Christ through the hope we have in him. Pope Francis himself embraces this symbol:

It is no coincidence that among the symbols of Christian hope there is one that I really like: *the anchor*. It expresses the notion that our hope is not vague; it is not to be confused with the uncertain sentiment of those who wish to improve the things of this world in an unrealistic way, relying only on their own willpower. Indeed, Christian hope is rooted not in the allure of the future, but in the *certainty of what God has promised us and accomplished in Jesus Christ*. If he guaranteed he would never abandon us, if every vocation begins with a "Follow me", with which he assures us he is always before us, why should we be afraid? With this promise, Christians can walk everywhere. Even passing through parts of the wounded world, where things are not going well, we are among those who still continue to hope. The Psalm says: "Even though I walk through the valley of the shadow of death, I fear no evil; for thou art with me"…It is precisely where darkness is rife that a light must be kept burning. Let us return to the anchor. Our faith is the anchor in heaven. We have anchored our life in heaven. What do we have to do? Hold fast to the rope: it is always there. And we go forward because we are certain that our life has an anchor in heaven, on that shore where we will arrive.[33]

Mary's grace-filled acceptance of this request from God did not mean she had an easy passage through life. No doubt she had temptations, as did her Son, though she was able to resist - as he did, through his divine strength. But surely her strength and hope were sorely tested as she experienced what it meant to be the Mother of God. We can wonder what she had planned for the birth of this Child - surely not an unexpected and cold journey to Bethlehem with no place to stay when she arrived. Surely she didn't expect to flee from her own country and not return to Nazareth for some while, living in fear and perhaps hardship. We know she didn't fully understand when Our Lord had to be about his Father's business in the Temple, but we hear of her hope in him at the wedding feast (*Jn* 2:3-5), and we know she came to speak with him during his ministry (*Mt* 12:46), though whether she came to plead with him we do not know. Certainly she followed him as his ministry progressed, even to the foot of the cross. How it was that she could stand there as her Son died, still anchored in the hope of God's promises, can only be understood in the light of her trust in the Holy Spirit and her hope in God. Pope Francis expresses it thus:

> The image of Mary standing at the foot of the cross and grieving the death of her innocent Son has inspired artists of every age to present her as a model of persevering hope in God's promises. That hope was the fruit of a life of prayer and daily effort to be conformed to God's will, and was fulfilled in Jesus' rising to new life. As Mother of Hope, may Our Lady remain at our side, sustain us by her prayers and guide our steps as we seek to follow her Son every day of our lives.[34]

In this season of Advent, we are called to expand the horizons of our hearts, to be amazed by the life which presents itself each day with newness. In order to do this, we must learn to not depend on our own certainties, on our own established strategies, because the Lord comes at a time that we do not imagine. He comes to bring us into a more beautiful and grand dimension.

May Our Lady, the Virgin of Advent, help us not to consider ourselves proprietors of our life, not to resist when the Lord comes to change it, but to be ready to let ourselves be visited by him, the awaited and welcome guest, even if it disturbs our plans.[35]

### Points to ponder

- Mary believed. She already hoped and believed and was therefore open to the message the Angel brought, and she did not doubt the message, but continued to trust in God. Her question, so similar to that of Zechariah, is not that of a person looking for proof, but that of someone seeking to know how better to co-operate with God's plan. What are our questions of God this Advent? Are we doubtful of God's power and love for us and so must wait for a sign, and another, and another before we trust? Or do we say to God, "How shall this be?" and then wait in joyful hope for God to show us how it will be, with the awe and wonder of a child who knows his Father can do anything?

- How can we share the "hope that is in us"[36] with those who are losing hope? How can we, like Mary, "arise and go with haste", because, as Pope Francis says, "the world cannot wait". This Advent, can we do something practical to help those for whom hope is a very far-away light on the horizon?

- Ask yourself whether you are prepared at least to follow Pope Francis's exhortation: "[W]e must pray, that each day God may give us hope and give it to everyone: that hope which arises when we see God in the crib in Bethlehem. The message of the Good News entrusted to us is urgent. We too must run like the messenger on the mountains, because the world cannot wait, humanity is hungry and thirsty for justice, truth, peace."[37]

# HOPE OF THE CHURCH - THIRD WEEK OF ADVENT

## Prayers and readings

Grant, almighty God,
that looking forward in faith to the feast
of our Lord's birth,
we may feel all the happiness our Saviour brings
and celebrate his coming with unfailing joy.
Through our Lord Jesus Christ, your Son,
who lives and reigns with you and the Holy Spirit,
one God, for ever and ever.

*(Morning Prayer, third Sunday of Advent)*

Sing aloud, O daughter of Zion;
shout, O Israel!
Rejoice and exult with all your heart,
O daughter of Jerusalem!
The Lord has taken away the judgements against you,
he has cast out your enemies.
The King of Israel, the Lord, is in your midst;
you shall fear evil no more.

*(Zp 3:14-15)*

All-powerful God, increase our strength of will for doing good that Christ may find an eager welcome at his coming and call us to his side in the kingdom of heaven, where he lives and reigns with you and the Holy Spirit, one God, for ever and ever. Amen.[38]

Lord, her watch Thy Church is keeping:
when shall earth Thy rule obey?
When shall end the night of weeping?
When shall break the promised day?
See the whitening harvest languish,
waiting still the labourers' toil;
was it vain, Thy Son's deep anguish?
Shall the strong retain the spoil?

(*Henry Downton*)

## The Church - cradle of hope

The one mediator, Christ, established and ever sustains here on earth his holy Church, the community of faith, hope, and charity, as a visible organisation through which he communicates truth and grace to all men. (*CCC*, 771[39])

With the return of Our Lord to heaven, we could not blame the disciples if they had despaired, given up and gone their separate ways, putting down the previous three years to 'experience' and recounting the things they had seen and heard with an increasingly 'did that really happen?' mindset as the years passed. However, that is not what they did. What they saw and heard in the days and weeks following the Resurrection impelled them to continue in the hope that had been established in them. The time between the Resurrection and Pentecost became a kind of Advent for them as they prepared to let go of the presence of Jesus in the way they knew, and waited for the coming of the Holy Spirit. We do not hear a great deal about what happened in that forty days of waiting before the Ascension, but what we do hear is important as it is in these days that the embryonic hope that was in the Apostles was nurtured until it could be given birth at Pentecost.

> To them he presented himself alive after his Passion by many proofs, appearing to them during forty days, and speaking of the kingdom of God. (*Ac* 1:3)

We hear that there are "many proofs" which Jesus allowed his disciples to receive. Sometimes Our Lord seems disapproving of those who want faith confirmed by a sign; when the Pharisees and Sadducees asked him for a sign, he replied, "An evil and adulterous generation seeks for a sign, but no sign shall be given to it except the sign of Jonah" (*Mt* 16:4). However, the proofs he gives to his disciples in this 'advent' before Pentecost are not given to convert a group of cynical doubters, but to nourish and cultivate the hope that was in their hearts. The joy of the Resurrection is not a self-contained experience, but the foundation and hope of the future Church, and it is essential in these early days that the disciples are grounded in that reality. So there are "many proofs" and many appearances during those days, to prevent any doubt in the days of persecution to follow. We cannot help but wonder if Peter was thinking of this time when he wrote, "Always be prepared to make a defence to anyone who calls you to account for the hope that is in you, yet do it with gentleness and reverence" (*1 P* 3:15).

Proofs and appearances are not all that happened in that time before the Ascension. We are told that, as well as appearing to his disciples, Jesus was "speaking of the Kingdom of God" to them. So those days were a time in which Jesus was able to speak to his disciples from a new perspective, and they were surely able to hear his words with clearer minds, knowing him to be God in a way they had not understood before, though not without the vestiges of their previous hope, that he would yet prove to be the kind of Messiah who would free them from Roman rule (cf. *Ac* 1:6).

These precious days with the Lord before his Ascension must surely have been a time of great joy and hope. Pope Francis[40] points us to the words of the prophet Isaiah:

Thrills the barren desert with rejoicing; the wilderness takes heart, and blossoms, fair as the lily. Blossom on blossom, it will rejoice and sing for joy; all the majesty of Lebanon is bestowed on it, all the grace of Carmel and of Saron. All alike shall see the glory of the Lord, the majesty of our God. Stiffen, then, the sinews of drooping hand and flagging knee; give word to the faint-hearted: Take courage, and have no fear; see where your Lord is bringing redress for your wrongs, God himself, coming to deliver you! (*Is* 35:1-4)[41]

### Pentecost - birth of the world's hope

The time came when the disciples were called to watch Jesus depart from them in the form to which they were accustomed. By this time, their faith must have been firm and their hearts full of hope as they returned to Jerusalem. We find that they are not idle in the remaining days before Pentecost. Three points are evident from Acts 1:4, 14.

1.  They were *obedient*, returning to Jerusalem as the Lord had told them.

2.  They were *not alone* - they were with each other, and they were with Mary their Mother, given to them, and to us, by Jesus from the cross.

3.  They were *praying* earnestly - they "devoted themselves to prayer".

From this firm base of obedience, communion and prayer, Peter was called to one more task before the descent of the

Holy Spirit - the election of a replacement for Judas. With the election of Matthias, the community was prepared for the fulfilment of their great hope - the coming of the Paraclete, the Comforter, the Advocate, who would be the one to lead them into all truth as Jesus had promised (*Jn* 16:13). Again, we notice an 'Ecclesial' pattern here as they wait:

- The disciples, about 120 of them by now, were already under the leadership of Peter: "In those days Peter stood up among the brethren…" (*Ac* 1:15).

- Scripture is known and called upon: "Brethren, the scripture had to be fulfilled, which the Holy Spirit spoke beforehand by the mouth of David, concerning Judas who was guide to those who arrested Jesus" (*Ac* 1:16, probably referring to *Ps* 41:9 and 69:25).

- The company prayed before casting lots.

The disciples were preparing themselves for the arrival of a Person - just as Mary and Joseph had prepared themselves for the arrival of the child Jesus. We cannot help but wonder what Our Lady's thoughts and memories were as she helped the disciples ready themselves for this new Advent.

Pope Francis reminds us that an important theme of Advent is the visit of the Lord to humanity.

> The first visit - we all know - occurred with the Incarnation, Jesus' birth in the cave of Bethlehem; the second takes place in the present: the Lord visits us constantly, each day, walking alongside us and being a consoling presence; in the end, there will be the third, the last visit, which we proclaim each time that we recite the Creed: "He will come again in glory to judge the living and the dead".[42]

Pentecost too was a visit of the Lord to humanity, for which the disciples prepared, but this is a visit that has no ending. There is no time when the Holy Spirit is not with us, guiding, comforting and strengthening the Church.

After Pentecost we find the Church living under the guidance of the Holy Spirit in these four aspects:

> They devoted themselves to the apostles' teaching and fellowship, to the breaking of bread and the prayers. (*Ac* 2:42)

These four properties are still very much part of the Church today and form the core of her structure. We still hear the *Apostles' teaching*, not only in Scripture, particularly in the liturgy, but also in our bishops' understanding of and defence of the faith when questions arise. This teaching is encapsulated in the *Catechism of the Catholic Church* and articulated by the Pope and bishops throughout the world.

We still live in *fellowship*, in the communion of saints which we proclaim in the Apostles' Creed as part of their teaching, in which all those members of the Body of Christ, living now, or passed on to Purgatory and Heaven, pray for and support each other in communion with Christ the Head and endeavour to live their lives under the guidance of the Apostles' moral teaching.

Within this communion we celebrate the sacraments, most especially the Eucharist, or '*breaking of bread*', which sustains our life in Christ and is the "source and summit" of the Church's life (*CCC*, 1324).

Also within this communion we lead our life of *prayer*, most importantly within the liturgy, but also as individual members of Christ's Body the Church.

The Lord leads all persons by paths and in ways pleasing to him, and each believer responds according to his heart's resolve and the personal expressions of his prayer. However, Christian Tradition has retained three major expressions of prayer: vocal, meditative, and contemplative. They have one basic trait in common: composure of heart. This vigilance in keeping the Word and dwelling in the presence of God makes these three expressions intense times in the life of prayer. (*CCC*, 2699)

## Hope in Scripture

We notice how Pope Francis, the successor of Peter, also draws on the treasures of Scripture to help us in our Advent preparations. He refers frequently to Isaiah 52, which contains some of the most beautiful and comforting passages in the Old Testament:

> Awake, awake, put on your strength, O Zion;
> put on your beautiful garments…
> How beautiful upon the mountains
> are the feet of him who brings good tidings,
> who publishes peace, who brings good tidings of good,
> who publishes salvation,
> who says to Zion, "Your God reigns".
> Hark, your watchmen lift up their voice,
> together they sing for joy;
> for eye to eye they see
> the return of the Lord to Zion.
> Break forth together into singing,
> you waste places of Jerusalem;
> for the Lord has comforted his people,
> he has redeemed Jerusalem.
> The Lord has bared his holy arm
> before the eyes of all the nations;
> and all the ends of the earth shall see
> the salvation of our God. (*Is* 52:1, 7-10)

This passage is about the end of the Babylonian Exile. The country is ravaged, many of the people who had been captured and led into exile have died, many others have settled in the new country and accepted other gods. There is only a small remnant left who are faithful to the One God, and it is to this small remnant that Isaiah addresses his words. This passage is, Pope Francis tells us, a "Song of Exultation" by Jerusalem - and we are reminded of Hannah's song, of Miriam's and of Deborah's, and of Our Lady's Magnificat.

> It is a very important historic moment...[I]t is the opportunity for Israel to rediscover God and, in faith, rediscover itself. The Lord is near, and the "remnant", that is, the small population which survived the Exile and whose faith endured while in exile, which had undergone crises and continued to believe and hope even in the midst of darkness, that "remnant" will be able to see the wonders of God.[43]

Advent is our opportunity to rediscover God and our faith as we discern the nearness of the Lord in the Incarnation. We too are like a "faithful remnant"; many we knew have died or remained in exile, and sometimes the darkness has seemed great to us.

The history within Scripture of God's people, both before the Incarnation and in the initial days of the Church, is a rich treasury of hope for us in these days of Advent.

[T]he Church, especially during Advent and Lent and above all at the Easter Vigil, re-reads and re-lives the great events of salvation history in the "today" of her liturgy. (*CCC*, 1095)

We are presented with the events leading to our salvation so that we can better understand how these events prepared God's people to understand his coming at the Incarnation, and the life of the Church, showing us how the mystery of Christ is prefigured in the words of the Old Testament.

We may find ourselves leading a kind of 'double life' in Advent; in Church we hear of the expected second coming of Christ at the end of time, of the preparation of the people by John the Baptist for Christ's ministry and presence among them, and of the Annunciation to Mary. We may be urged to exercise restraint and remain sober and watchful for the coming of the Lord whilst rejoicing in his promises. Our churches remain undecorated and the vestments are mostly purple; there is a general air of quiet waiting and expectation until Christmas Eve arrives. Once outside the building, however, everything is different. The streets and windows of our homes are ablaze with light and ornaments. The shops are loaded with decorations and gifts and constant Christmas music is piped out. Often we are expected to attend Christmas parties and concerts and to dress accordingly. We have to live in both these worlds during Advent; we are the "remnant" in observing Advent with the Church, and the remnant who celebrate Christmas with the Church, the remnant who look forward to the final visit of Jesus to humanity at the end of time.

> When the Church celebrates *the liturgy of Advent* each year, she makes present this ancient expectancy of the Messiah, for by sharing in the long preparation for the Saviour's first coming, the faithful renew their ardent desire for his second coming. By celebrating the precursor's birth and martyrdom, the Church unites herself to his desire: "He must increase, but I must decrease." (*CCC*, 524)

Pope Francis reminds us of how this should affect our lives:

> From this perspective there also comes an invitation to sobriety, to not be controlled by the things of this world, by material reality, but rather to govern them. If, by contrast, we allow ourselves to be influenced and overpowered by these things, we cannot perceive that there is something very important: our final encounter with the Lord: this is important. That encounter. And everyday matters must have this horizon, and must be directed to that horizon.[44]

In the midst of our rejoicing, as we lead our 'double life' through Advent, this horizon is where we should fix our eyes. We are children of hope, inheritors of that first hope given to the Church at Pentecost, and we have a horizon of hope to guide us. We must always be ready to put down the glitter and allure of the world and go out and meet the Lord. Pope Francis advises:

> In this season of Advent, we are called to expand the horizons of our hearts, to be amazed by the life which presents itself each day with newness. In order to do this, we must learn to not depend on our own certainties, on our own established strategies, because the Lord comes at a time that we do not imagine. He comes to bring us into a more beautiful and grand dimension.[45]

According to the *Catechism*, we therefore have a great need today of catechesis, to "help the faithful to open themselves to this spiritual understanding of the economy of salvation as the Church's liturgy reveals it and enables us to live it." (*CCC*, 1095)

### Points to ponder

This Advent, we might consider our relationship with the Church.

- Am I obedient to what Jesus has taught through his Church, or am I going my own way if it suits me?

- Am I seeking the support of Mary and the saints, and of our own brothers and sisters in faith, or trying to be Christian on my own?

- Am I devoting myself to prayer - or is this something that gets overlooked unless I am in great need?

# HOPE FOR THE WORLD - FOURTH WEEK OF ADVENT

### Prayers and readings

Pour forth, we beseech you, O Lord,
your grace into our hearts,
that we, to whom the Incarnation of Christ your Son
was made known by the message of an Angel,
may by his Passion and Cross
be brought to the glory of his Resurrection.
Who lives and reigns with you in the unity
of the Holy Spirit,
one God, for ever and ever.

*(Collect for the fourth Sunday of Advent;
prayed also after the Angelus)*

You heavens, send dew from above, you skies, pour down
upon us the rain we long for, him, the Just One; may he,
the Saviour, spring from the closed womb of earth, and
with him let right order take its being.

*(Is 45:8, Douay-Rheims version)*

*Truth has arisen from the earth and justice has looked down from heaven*

Awake, mankind! For your sake God has become man. Awake, you who sleep, rise up from the dead, and Christ will enlighten you. I tell you again: for your sake, God became man.

You would have suffered eternal death, had he not been born in time. Never would you have been freed from sinful flesh, had he not taken on himself the likeness of sinful flesh. You would have suffered everlasting unhappiness, had it not been for this mercy. You would never have returned to life, had he not shared your death. You would have been lost if he had not hastened to your aid. You would have perished, had he not come.

*(From a sermon by St Augustine, Office of Readings, fourth Sunday of Advent)*

Now to him who is able to strengthen you according to my gospel and the preaching of Jesus Christ, according to the revelation of the mystery which was kept secret for long ages but is now disclosed and through the prophetic writings is made known to all nations, according to the command of the eternal God, to bring about the obedience of faith - to the only wise God be glory for evermore through Jesus Christ! Amen.

*(Second Reading for the fourth Sunday of Advent: Rm 16:25-27)*

### Christian hope in the world

When we speak of hope, often it refers to what is not in man's power to realise, which is invisible. In fact, what we hope for goes beyond our strength and our perception. But the Birth of Christ, inaugurating redemption, speaks to us of a different hope, a dependable, visible and understandable hope, because it is founded in God.[46]

Pope Francis here refers to the way most people tend to use the term 'hope'. We hope it will be a fine day for the picnic, or that our team will win the match - and perhaps both these hopes come more into the category of wishful thinking! Or perhaps we hope the baby will be born healthy or that a young man will be cured of his illness. However, although we can make predictions based on scientific observations, this plays no part in what is in our hearts and is beyond our control. Our hopes lie forever beyond our powers. The loss of such hopes causes us the most grief; those couples who wish for a child may never have their hopes fulfilled and may grieve for a lifetime, but those who have decided against welcoming children have no such hopes to be dashed.

Christian hope, so potent in the season of Advent, is neither wishful thinking nor unfulfilled desire. The writer of the Letter to the Hebrews puts it this way:

> Now faith is the assurance of things hoped for, the conviction of things not seen. (*Heb* 1:11)

This "assurance of things hoped for" is grounded in faith; but it does not mean that our own faith is the foundation of our hope; we should soon be in a state of collapse if that were so. It is the faith of the Church, the faith given to us through Jesus Christ, the faith to which we hold with both our own weak efforts and with the mighty strength and grace of God who comes to help us, which is the assurance of our hope. St Paul points out that this hope that is in us is as yet still unseen - or it could not be called hope - but nevertheless, we wait patiently for our redemption:

> We know that the whole creation has been groaning in travail together until now; and not only the creation, but we ourselves, who have the first fruits of the Spirit, groan inwardly as we wait for adoption as sons, the redemption of our bodies. For in this hope we were saved. Now hope that is seen is not hope. For who hopes for what he sees? But if we hope for what we do not see, we wait for it with patience. (*Rm* 8:22-25)

As Pope Francis puts it, "Thus for a Christian, to hope means the certainty of being on a journey with Christ toward the Father who awaits us",[47] and as the *Catechism* enlightens us further:

> When God reveals Himself and calls him, man cannot fully respond to the divine love by his own powers. He must hope that God will give him the capacity to love Him in return and to act in conformity with the commandments of charity. Hope is the confident expectation of divine blessing and the beatific vision of God; it is also the fear of offending God's love and of incurring punishment. (*CCC*, 2090)

So this "certainty" is not to be confused with the sins against hope of despair and presumption:

> By *despair*, man ceases to hope for his personal salvation from God, for help in attaining it or for the forgiveness of his sins. Despair is contrary to God's goodness, to his justice - for the Lord is faithful to his promises - and to his mercy.
>
> There are two kinds of *presumption*. Either man presumes upon his own capacities (hoping to be able to save himself without help from on high), or he presumes upon God's almighty power or his mercy (hoping to obtain his forgiveness without conversion and glory without merit). (*CCC*, 2090-2092)

This, then, is our Christian hope, that God, in his great mercy, will provide the grace for us to live in hope of salvation. However, as the *Catechism* reminds us:

> The world we live in often seems very far from the one promised us by faith. Our experiences of evil and suffering, injustice and death, seem to contradict the Good News; they can shake our faith and become a temptation against it. (*CCC*, 164)

We are urged to remind ourselves of the great "cloud of witnesses" (*Heb* 12:1), "Abraham, who 'in hope...believed against hope'; ...the Virgin Mary, who, in 'her pilgrimage of faith', walked into the 'night of faith' in sharing the darkness of her son's suffering and death; and... so many others" (*CCC*, 165).

## Hope for the world

Pope Francis reminds us that, "walking in this world, with hope, we are saved".[48] But what of those who do not walk with our hope? How are they to see Advent as a season of hope and not simply an anticipation of excess? Christian hope cannot be forced upon people, nor can it be manufactured in hearts that are closed to the Lord and unwilling to consider the Incarnation in any way. Our Western, post-Christian culture does not have a lot of references left concerning the real meaning of Christmas, but it is not entirely bereft of its heritage, and it is these vestiges which we can use to spread the seeds of the Gospel.

Pope Francis guides us here:

> In Christian homes, during the Season of Advent, the Nativity scene is arranged, according to the tradition which dates back to St Francis of Assisi. In its simple way, the Nativity scene conveys hope; each one of the characters is immersed in this atmosphere of hope.[49]

Almost everyone is familiar with the Nativity scene; many homes have a crib on display and it is still not unusual to see the Nativity scene arranged in a shop window or a town centre. Most people will still retain a sense of respect for this, or a sentimental attachment of some kind. A young mother visiting my house one Christmas was horrified when her young child picked up one of the wise men to play with, but this provided an opportunity to build on the idea that many people have about "Christmas being for the children" and to ponder why we focus so much on children and gifts at this time. Her innate sense of respect and propriety was well founded; though she had never had any Christian input as a child herself, she still retained a kind of reverence for something she saw as 'holy'.[50]

Pope Francis takes us through the Nativity scene, showing us the deeper meaning of some of its parts and how they are rooted in the history of Israel which flowered in the Virgin Mary. He notes first the place where Jesus was born: Bethlehem, which means "house of bread". Many people have pointed out that, "The name…'Bethlehem' is so significant that one can't help but recognise the obvious fact that Jesus' birth in Bethlehem is the work of God the Father. In Hebrew, 'Bethlehem' means 'House of Bread'. The little town of Bethlehem is the house where we find Jesus, the Bread of Life. It is where God becomes food for mankind. And in Aramaic, 'Bethlehem' means 'House of Flesh'. The little town of Bethlehem is the house where the Incarnation, the Word of God becoming flesh, takes place. It is where God becomes man."[51]

Pope Francis points out:

> In this way, he seems to tell us that he is born as bread for us; he enters our life to give us his life; he comes into our world to give us his love. He does not come to devour or to lord it over us, but instead to feed and serve us. There is a straight line between the manger and the cross where Jesus will become bread that is broken. It is the straight line of love that gives and saves, the love that brings light to our lives and peace to our hearts.[52]

The Holy Father also notes the theme of Kingship, as Bethlehem was the place where, so many years before, David the shepherd boy was born, he who would become King of Israel. Jesus himself is born from that royal line; he is the Son of David, and he is also the Good Shepherd who watches over his sheep and knows them all by name.

Bethlehem's significance lies in that connection, not in its greatness, for it was a humble place, chosen by God who "loves to act through the little ones and the humble".[53] Jesus, son of David, king and shepherd, and Jesus, Son of God, unites in his own person the hopes of earth and heaven.

Next, Pope Francis considers Mary, referring to her as "Mother of Hope" who opened the door of our world to God. He also refers to her being, for nine months, "the Ark of the new and eternal Covenant".[54] This idea of understanding Mary as the "Ark of the Covenant" is not new,[55] but is a very beautiful and profound means of expressing her holiness and that of the child she carried in her womb. The article and book cited below give more detail on Mary as the Ark of the New Covenant but, briefly, here are the connections which arise naturally from the clear links within Scripture.

- The old Ark of the Covenant was the place where the glory of God - the *Shekinah* - dwelled. Mary, the New Ark, the place where God chose to dwell at the start of the Incarnation, is the new dwelling place of God. The instructions given for the making of the old Ark were very specific, and indicate the perfection require by God;[56] thus we should not be surprised that Mary also is made perfect in order to be the dwelling place of God. Instead of a beautifully made - but wooden - vessel, we have a perfect human woman.

- The old Ark contained three things, according to the writer of the Letter to the Hebrews: "a golden urn holding the manna, and Aaron's rod that budded, and the tables of the covenant" (*Heb* 9:1-4). Mary also held within her the living Bread of Life, the great high priest and the Word of God.

- Mary's visit to Elizabeth, where the unborn John the Baptist "leaped for joy" in the womb of Elizabeth (*Lk* 1:41), was a clear fulfilment for the early Church Fathers of when King David "arose and went" to the hill country of Judah and brought back the Ark, leaping and dancing with joy before the Lord (*2 Sam* 6).

- In the Revelation of St John, the Ark of the Covenant is again seen in the Temple - though it had been missing for many centuries, having been hidden by Jeremiah in order to protect it from the Babylonian invaders.[57] But immediately after this, John goes on to describe not a gilded wooden box, but a woman, "clothed with the sun, with the moon under her feet, and on her head a crown of twelve stars" (*Rv* 12:1);[58] the old Ark had been lost, but Mary, the Ark of the New Covenant, is now our Mother and our Queen.

All that we understand about Mary is directed to one end, to our becoming closer to her Son, so as we contemplate the idea of Mary as Ark of the Covenant this Advent, we find we are drawn nearer to Christ. Those things which we find prefigured in the Old Testament become perfected in the New, so that we are more able, through Mary, to understand the Person of her Son.

The next figure in the Nativity scene considered by Pope Francis is St Joseph, who contemplates the child in the manger; surely, Pope Francis implies, he is thinking of the Holy Spirit who is the true Father of this child. Pope Francis wonders if, as Joseph looks at the Child in the manger, he "reflects on the fact that that Child has come from the Holy Spirit, and that God himself commanded him to call [the Child] 'Jesus'".[59] St Joseph, the Pope also thinks, is considering the name he has been commanded to give the child:

> In that name there is hope for every man and woman, because through that son of woman, God will save mankind from death and from sin. This is why it is important to contemplate the Nativity scene![60]

The Bible does not record a single word spoken by St Joseph, yet he is given the significant task of naming the child born to Mary. St Joseph, of course, was faced with a terrible moral dilemma; he was both a "just man" - a righteous person - and a kind one, unwilling to put Mary through the shame (or worse) of a public denouncement (*Mt* 1:19). However, being "righteous" means following the commandments of God, however mysterious they may seem, and Joseph is obedient. He accepts the responsibility of naming the child, thereby taking him into his own family and giving him full hereditary rights and establishing him as his own adopted child. This is perhaps why Matthew goes to such pains to establish the genealogy of Joseph at the start of his Gospel.[61]

The name "Jesus", given by the angel to Joseph, means "The Lord saves". It is the equivalent of the Hebrew Joshua, which means the same, but whereas Joshua was to save his people by leading them into the Promised Land across the River Jordan, Jesus is to save his people from their sins and into the eternal rest of heaven. Matthew gives us another name also, "Emmanuel", which means "God with us". This is more than a name; it describes what is happening at the Incarnation and until the end of time. God is with us "always, to the close of the age" (*Mt* 18:20, 28:20), in his Church and in his Eucharistic presence.

Also in the Nativity scene are the shepherds, the "little ones". Pope Francis reminds us that these

> represent the humble and poor who await the Messiah, the "consolation of Israel" (*Lk* 2:25), and the "redemption of Jerusalem" (*Lk* 2:38). In this Child they see the realisation of the promises and hope that the salvation of God will finally arrive for each of them.[62]

The shepherds are not trusting in their own certainties about life and hope; indeed, they may have had very few certainties. Their occupation was frowned upon by some of the religious groups of the time, possibly because of its lowly status which had become inferior to farming as land ownership grew after the occupation of the Promised Land. Certainly by the time of Jesus, shepherds had neither high social status nor many civil rights. However, God had not forgotten the shepherds of the Old Testament upon whom he had called to proclaim his messages. The Bethlehem shepherds stood in solidarity with a long line of shepherds who listened to God and carried out his work; we remember Abel, Jacob, Joseph, Moses, David and Amos.[63] It was surely most fitting that the birth of Jesus, the long-hoped-for Lamb of God, should be first announced to shepherds - not only because of their low status and humility, but also because God wishes to say something to his people about the value and symbolism of the shepherd.

Pope Francis finally mentions the "choir of angels", though a Nativity scene is usually restricted to one angel, whose name is clearly "Gloria" as this is printed on the front of the garment! However, the very concept of angels can be a means of witness to the world. Although the West seems to have largely abandoned its religious practice, this has not destroyed the innate need for God and the yearning for some means of expressing this desire, unrecognised though it may be. Those who would say they have no faith and who would never be caught speaking of God, or of Christianity, nevertheless will often resort to language about angels, speaking of their guardian angels, or of a person who has died and whom they now consider to be an "angel in heaven". This expression of their hope, diminished and misguided though it may be, still indicates the eternal hope that lives in the human heart. For the Christian, our "hope is expressed in praise and gratitude to God, who has initiated his Kingdom of love, justice and peace".[64]

As we come to the end of Advent, let us reflect on the Nativity scene and its characters, before they are pushed aside for the serving of food and drink, or buried under used wrapping paper.

## Points to ponder

I too have an angel who watches over me - not in a sentimental or magical way, but who is sent by God to be the guardian of my soul. Do I acknowledge the presence of this heavenly helper and turn to him in prayer? As this Christmas turns to a New Year, may God help us to be more aware of this particular blessing he has given us.

- Angel of God, my guardian dear,
  To whom God's love commits me here,
  Ever this day (night) be at my side,
  To light and guard, to rule and guide.

- The shepherds, despised and marginalised, were the ones, Pope Francis reminds us, who "set out with haste" to see the Child Jesus while "[p]eople who felt sure of themselves, self-sufficient, were at home with their possessions."[65] Will we be like this at Christmas - content, happy with our possessions and unwilling perhaps to look at the situation of those who are not so fortunate? Or is there some way in which we too can "set out with haste" to see the Christ Child?

- St Joseph was called by God to do a most important task, yet we do not hear a word from him, we simply see his silent obedience. This Christmas, we too can reflect on the tasks and duties we are called to and the level of obedience we have given.

- Finally, as Advent turns to Christmas, let us consider our Blessed Lady, not, as some would see it, as a kind of alternative to Jesus, but as our Mother who leads us to her Son in his humble birth at Bethlehem. All that we learn about Mary, our Mother of Hope, and all the love and help we experience from her, to which so many can testify, is given us for one end only: that we may understand more fully how to receive God's grace in our souls and share the life of the Holy Trinity through her Son.

- Hail, holy Queen, Mother of mercy,
  hail, our life, our sweetness and our hope.
  To thee do we cry, poor banished children of Eve:
  to thee do we send up our sighs,
  mourning and weeping in this vale of tears.
  Turn then, most gracious Advocate,
  thine eyes of mercy toward us,
  and after this our exile,
  show unto us the blessed fruit of thy womb, Jesus,
  O merciful, O loving, O sweet Virgin Mary.
  Amen.

# Hope Fulfilled - Christmas

## Prayers and readings

Today the king of heaven has deigned to be born of a virgin for us, to recall fallen man to his heavenly kingdom. Hosts of angels rejoice, for eternal salvation has come to the human race. Glory to God in the highest, and on earth peace among men with whom he is well pleased.

*(Office of Readings for Christmas Day)*

*Christian, remember your dignity*
Dearly beloved, today our Saviour is born; let us rejoice. Sadness should have no place on the birthday of life. The fear of death has been swallowed up; life brings us joy with the promise of eternal happiness.

No one is shut out from this joy; all share the same reason for rejoicing. Our Lord, victor over sin and death, finding no man free from sin, came to free us all. Let the saint rejoice as he sees the palm of victory at hand. Let the sinner be glad as he receives the offer of forgiveness. Let the pagan take courage as he is summoned to life…

Christian, remember your dignity, and now that you share in God's own nature, do not return by sin to your former base condition. Bear in mind who is your head and of whose body you are a member. Do not forget that you have been rescued from the power of darkness and brought into the light of God's kingdom.

Through the sacrament of baptism you have become a temple of the Holy Spirit. Do not drive away so great a guest by evil conduct and become again a slave to the devil, for your liberty was bought by the blood of Christ.

*(From a sermon by Pope St Leo the Great,*
*Office of Readings for Christmas Day)*

O God, who wonderfully created
the dignity of human nature
and still more wonderfully restored it,
grant, we pray,
that we may share in the divinity of Christ,
who humbled himself to share in our humanity.
Who lives and reigns with you
in the unity of the Holy Spirit,
one God, for ever and ever.

*(Collect for Mass of Christmas Day)*

## Hope fulfilled

Christmas, when the Incarnation of our Lord, hidden in the womb of Mary for nine months, is revealed to the world, is the implementation of all the hope of humanity in the long ages since the Fall and the first hint of redemption. It is the realisation of Israel's longing for a Messiah-King who will save them from their enemies, though they did not then realise that the enemy is within and so salvation must also be internalised. It is the comprehension of Mary's place as the Daughter of Zion, the Flower of Israel and now Mother of Hope, prefigured by so many women to whom God called. It is the implementation of the hopes of the Apostles as they waited for and received the Holy Spirit and built up the Church, the Body of Christ, in the same hope with which she celebrates today. And it is the hope of the world, though the world confuses its beauty with baubles and its glory with glitter.

Pope Francis speaks of it in this way:

> It is a night of glory, that glory proclaimed by the angels in Bethlehem and by ourselves as well, all over the world. It is a night of joy, because henceforth and forever, the infinite and eternal God is God with us. He is not far off. We need not search for him in the heavens or in mystical notions. He is close at hand. He became man and he will never withdraw from our humanity, which he has made his own.[66]

This is a wonderful truth which the Holy Father has highlighted here. "He became man and he will never withdraw from our humanity, which he has made his own." Human nature is not something which Jesus took in order to live on earth with us, and then discarded at some point to return to heaven as a purely spiritual being. No, when the Word was made flesh and dwelt among us (*Jn* 1:14), he was made flesh forever. He has not discarded our human nature, *but has taken it with him into heaven*. One of our race dwells there with the Father and the Holy Spirit, and not only the Lord, but his Blessed Mother also, as he would not leave her behind. This is an amazing truth on which we can ponder at Christmas. This now is our hope; that we too will be in the presence of God, not as disembodied spirits, but, like our Blessed Lady, present to God in our full body-and-soul humanity. This is indeed a great hope, expressed already in the ancient book of Job:

> For I know that my Redeemer lives,
> and at last he will stand upon the earth;
> and after my skin has been thus destroyed,
> then from my flesh I shall see God.

(*Jb* 19:25-26)

However, although we have such a great hope, this does not absolve us from an awareness of those who live without hope, who suffer persecution for their hope or whose hopes are vested in those things which can never satisfy the deepest human needs. Pope Francis advises us here:

The new-born Child challenges us. He calls us to leave behind fleeting illusions and to turn to what is essential, to renounce our insatiable cravings, to abandon our endless yearning for things we will never have. We do well to leave such things behind, in order to discover, in the simplicity of the divine Child, peace, joy and the luminous meaning of life.[67]

He also confronts us with the reality of the Christmas season for many children:

Let us allow the Child in the manger to challenge us, but let us also be challenged by all those children in today's world who are lying not in a crib, caressed with affection by their mothers and fathers, but in squalid "mangers that devour dignity". Children who hide underground to escape bombardment, on the pavements of large cities, in the hold of a boat overladen with immigrants… Let us allow ourselves to be challenged by those children who are not allowed to be born, by those who cry because no one relieves their hunger, by those who hold in their hands not toys, but weapons.[68]

The first Christmas also was not without its challenges. The Holy Family were away from home, in unsuitable accommodation and unable to return to Nazareth for some time because of the political situation. And immediately after the joy of Christmas Day, within the Octave of Christmas, we find the Church recalling the memory of her first martyr, St Stephen, the deaths of the Holy Innocents and the murder of St Thomas Becket. Why does the Church recall these terrible events so close to the joy of Christmas?

> The mystery of Christmas, which is light and joy, challenges and unsettles us, because it is at once a mystery of hope and of sadness. It has a taste of sadness, inasmuch as love is not accepted, and life discarded.[69]

The time in which we live, the age of the Holy Spirit and the Church, is a time of tension. Unlike the previous ages, that of the Old Testament in which the Father was worshipped but the Holy Trinity was not yet revealed, and that of the Son in which the Second Person of that Trinity lived among us but "the world knew him not" (*Jn* 1:10), our present age is not yet complete. We rejoice in the fulfilment of the hopes of previous ages, especially in the Incarnation at Christmas time, but we live in close juxtaposition with persecution of Christians, terror attacks, widespread abortion and general scorn and unbelief - in an age of hope not yet fully realised. It was the same in the early days of the Church; the Holy Innocents lost their lives through the whim of a powerful ruler and Stephen died because he served and proclaimed Christ in a land where he was denied. As Pope Francis puts it, "The Protomartyr Stephen, full of the Holy Spirit, was stoned because he professed his faith in Jesus Christ, the Son of God."[70] Later, St Thomas Becket died for the sake of justice, holding his faith more dearly than his friendship with the King; whatever the historical intrigues surrounding the events, it is clear that he stood firm in his faith to the point of death, preferring the hope of eternal life to the favour of the King.

Pope Francis urges us to remember at Christmas those who are persecuted for their faith:

> Today too, in order to bear witness to light and to truth, the Church experiences, in different places, harsh persecution, up to the supreme sacrifice of martyrdom. How many of our brothers and sisters in faith endure abuse and violence, and are hated because of Jesus! I shall tell you something: today's martyrs are more numerous with respect to those of the first centuries. When we read the history of the first centuries, here in Rome, we read of so much cruelty toward Christians; I tell you: there is the same cruelty today, and to a greater extent, toward Christians. Today we should think of those who are suffering from persecution, and...be close to them with our affection, our prayers and also our tears.[71]

So, in the midst of our rejoicing, we remember, as the Church does, the sorrow and pain of her history. We remember, as our present Holy Father Pope Francis reminds us, that many Christians today are persecuted for political reasons, like Stephen and St Thomas were, and many children never come to birth. And we pray, as encouraged by Pope Francis, for joy and courage to continue in our faith - sustained always by hope, for Christ who comes to us at Christmas is the true Hope of the world.

In making room in our heart for the Son of God who gives himself to us at Christmas, let us joyfully and courageously renew the will to follow him faithfully, as the only guide, by continuing to live according to the Gospel attitude and rejecting the mentality of those who dominate this world.

Let us raise our prayers to the Virgin Mary, Mother of God and Queen of Martyrs, that she may guide us and always sustain us on our journey in following Jesus Christ, whom we contemplate in the grotto of the Nativity and who is the faithful Witness of God the Father.[72]

# Endnotes

[1] Pope Francis, General Audience, Paul VI Audience Hall, Wednesday 7th December 2016.

[2] Pope Francis, Angelus, Saint Peter's Square, Sunday 27th November 2016.

[3] Benedict XVI, *Spe Salvi*, 22.

[4] Pope Francis, Homily, Vatican Basilica, Midnight Mass, Solemnity of the Nativity of the Lord, Saturday 24th December 2016.

[5] A pastoral letter by St Charles Borromeo for the season of Advent.

[6] Pope Francis, General Audience, Paul VI Audience Hall, Wednesday 7th December 2016.

[7] "Gospel", of course, means "good news". This is the first good news: news of hope and expectation.

[8] Tradition tells us that Mary's mother was St Anne.

[9] St Bernard (1090-1153), sermon on the *"Missus est"*: https://archive.org/stream/ sermonsofstberna00bernuoft/ sermonsofstberna00bernuoft _djvu.txt

[10] Pope Francis, Angelus, Saint Peter's Square, Solemnity of the Immaculate Conception of the Blessed Virgin Mary, Thursday 8th December 2016.

[11] Pope Francis, General Audience, Paul VI Audience Hall, Wednesday 7th December 2016.

[12] More recently the symbol of the rainbow has been adopted by those who support same sex relationships. Again we can see the evidence of the Fall in this disordered hope. While it is good to support the idea that no-one should be persecuted for their sexual orientation and hope for a kinder understanding of their difficulties, we must still acknowledge that such relationships hold no hope for the future as they are necessarily barren.

[13] Pope Francis, General Audience, Paul VI Audience Hall, Wednesday 28th December 2016.

[14] Pope Francis, Angelus, Saint Peter's Square, Solemnity of the Immaculate Conception of the Blessed Virgin Mary, Thursday 8th December 2016.

[15] Pope Francis, General Audience, Paul VI Audience Hall, Wednesday 7th December 2016.

[16] Ibid.

[17] Ibid.

[18] Ibid.

[19] Prayer partially based on Pope Francis's teaching after the Angelus, Saint Peter's Square, Sunday 11th December 2016.

[20] Cardinal John Henry Newman, "The Glories of Mary for the Sake of Her Son", in his *Discourses Addressed to Mixed Congregations*, 344 (widely cited on the internet and available at *http://www.newmanreader.org/works/discourses/discourse17.html* ).

[21] From the Novena to Our Lady of Hope: *http://www.ewtn.com/devotionals/novena/hope.htm*

[22] Passionist nuns: *https://www.passionistnuns.org/meditation/MCMShuhmann/index.htm*

[23] From "Eve and Mary" in the treatise *Against Heresies* by St Irenaeus.

[24] Pope Francis, General Audience, Paul VI Audience Hall, Wednesday 7th December 2016.

[25] Pope Francis, Angelus, Saint Peter's Square, Solemnity of the Immaculate Conception of the Blessed Virgin Mary, Thursday 8th December 2016.

[26] Ibid.

[27] Ibid.

[28] Pope Francis, General Audience, Saint Peter's Square, Wednesday 5th April 2017.

[29] Benedict XVI, *Deus Caritas Est*, 1.

[30] Ibid., 41.

[31] Pope Francis, Angelus, Saint Peter's Square, Solemnity of the Immaculate Conception of the Blessed Virgin Mary, Thursday 8th December 2016.

[32] Pope Francis, General Audience, Wednesday 21st December 2016.

[33] Pope Francis, General Audience, Saint Peter's Square, Wednesday 26th April 2017.

[34] Pope Francis, General Audience, Wednesday 10th May 2017.

[35] Pope Francis, Angelus, Saint Peter's Square, Sunday 27th November 2016.

[36] "Always be prepared to make a defence to anyone who calls you to account for the hope that is in you, yet do it with gentleness and reverence; and keep your conscience clear, so that, when you are abused, those who revile your good behaviour in Christ may be put to shame" (*1 P* 3:15-16).

[37] Pope Francis, General Audience, Paul VI Audience Hall, Wednesday, 14th December 2016.

[38] *http://www.catholic.org/prayers/prayer.php?p=352*

[39] Quoting from *Lumen Gentium*, 184.

[40] Pope Francis, Angelus, Saint Peter's Square, Sunday 11th December 2016.

[41] Pope Francis uses a modern translation here, but I have chosen the older Douai-Rheims version for this quotation because of the great beauty of the language.

[42] Pope Francis, Angelus, Saint Peter's Square, Sunday 27th November 2016.

[43] Pope Francis, General Audience, Paul VI Audience Hall, Wednesday 14th December 2016.

[44] Pope Francis, Angelus, Saint Peter's Square, Sunday 27th November 2016.

[45] Ibid.

[46] Pope Francis, General Audience, Paul VI Audience Hall, Wednesday 21st December 2016.

[47] Ibid.

[48] Ibid.

[49] Ibid.

[50] It was difficult to smooth over her mortification when the young lad dropped the Wise Man and his head broke off!

[51] *http://loweryournets.blogspot.co.uk/2010/12/house-of-bread-house-of-flesh.html*

[52] Pope Francis, General Audience, Paul VI Audience Hall, Wednesday 21st December 2016.

[53] Ibid.

[54] Ibid.

[55] St Gregory Thaumaturgus (*c.*213-*c.*270) makes an early reference to this concept: "The ark is verily the holy Virgin, gilded within and without, who received the treasure of universal sanctification. Arise, O Lord, from the Father's bosom, to raise up again the ruined race of our first parent" (*Orat. in Deip. Annunciat. Int. Opp. S. Greg. Thaumaturg*) (Blessed Virgin, 89): *https://stpeterslist.com/4-biblical-reasons-mary-is-the-new-ark-of-the-covenant*. See also Scott Hahn, *Hail Holy Queen: The Mother of God in the Word of God*, Darton, Longman and Todd, London, 2001, ch. 3 and *Ignatius Catholic Study Bible* (Luke), Ignatius Press, San Francisco, 2001, 21.

[56] "And let them make me a sanctuary, that I may dwell in their midst" (*Ex* 25:8).
Look particularly at Exodus 25:10-22 to see the precise details given for the Ark's construction.

[57] "And Jeremiah came and found a cave, and he brought there the tent and the ark and the altar of incense, and he sealed up the entrance. Some of those who followed him came up to mark the way, but could not find it. When Jeremiah learned of it, he rebuked them and declared: 'The place shall be unknown until God gathers his people together again and shows his mercy'" (*2 Mac* 2:5-8).

[58] We should remember here that the organisation of Scripture into chapter and verse is a relatively new arrangement; the Bible did not originally have such divisions. Stephen Langton, Archbishop of Canterbury in the thirteenth century, added the chapters, and a French printer called Robert Stephanus added the verses in the sixteenth century.

[59] Pope Francis, General Audience, Paul VI Audience Hall, Wednesday 21st December 2016.

[60] Ibid.

[61] We should note the inclusion of women in the genealogy here. These are not the women earlier referred to (with the exception of Ruth), but are irregular in lifestyle and origin. Ruth was a foreigner; Bathsheba, the wife of Uriah, was an adulteress; Rahab was a prostitute; and Tamar was raped and thus permanently disgraced by her brother who was not even punished for it by her father, King David. "By listing the immoral women in the generations before Solomon, Matthew implies that if these women did not disqualify

Solomon as the royal son of David, then neither do they disqualify Jesus, who assumes the same title as the Messiah. *Mt* 1:1": *Ignatius Catholic Study Bible* (Matthew), Ignatius Press, San Francisco, 1999, 17.

[62] Pope Francis, General Audience, Paul VI Audience Hall, Wednesday 21st December 2016.

[63] *Ignatius Catholic Study Bible* (Luke), Ignatius Press, San Francisco, 2001, 22.

[64] Pope Francis, General Audience, Paul VI Audience Hall, Wednesday 21st December 2016.

[65] Pope Francis, Homily, Vatican Basilica, Solemnity of the Nativity of the Lord, Papal Mass, Saturday 24th December 2016.

[66] Ibid.

[67] Ibid.

[68] Ibid.

[69] Ibid.

[70] Pope Francis, Angelus, Saint Peter's Square, Feast of St Stephen, Protomartyr, Monday 26th December 2016.

[71] Ibid.

[72] Ibid.